C000125373

NORTHUMBRIA

By the same author

Teach Yourself Photography
The Question and Answer Guide to Photo Techniques
Taking Pictures for Profit: The Complete Guide to Selling Your Work
The A–Z of Creative Photography
Lee Frost's Personal Views: The Art of Colour Landscape Photography

NORTHUMBRIA

LEE FROST

with an introduction by

ERIC ROBSON

Constable · London

First published in Great Britain 1998 by Constable, an imprint of Constable & Robinson Ltd
3 The Lanchesters, 162 Fulham Palace Road, London W6 9ER
Copyright © Lee Frost 1998, Introduction Copyright © Eric Robson 1998
ISBN 0 09 477410 2
The right of Lee Frost to be identified as author of this work has been
asserted by him in accordance with the Copyright, Designs and Patents Act 1988

Reprinted 2001

Printed in Hong Kong through World Print Ltd

A CIP catalogue record for this book
is available from the British Library

For Julie and Noah

*The author would like to thank the National Trust for Northumbria,
the Northumberland National Park authorities and English Heritage
for their co-operation in the making of this book*

CONTENTS

The high clouds are piling across the years from the west and I'm having to lean hard into a moaning and blustering wind. This is High Warden Hill near Hexham, two acres of hill fort that in southern Britain would be described as Iron Age. But prehistorians have said that this northern region was altogether too backward to have one of those; that it passed from the rough settlements of Beaker-folk and workers of bronze to the all mod cons of the *Pax Romana*, missing the bits in between. Frankly, I don't believe them for the simple reason that Northumbrians are altogether too canny and inventive to have allowed the opportunities of something as useful as iron to be the preserve of soft southerners. So let's agree that it's Iron Age at least in spirit, whatever the experts say.

We're high above the sheltered valley of the River Tyne, first explored and settled by groups of hunter-fisher folk in the middle Stone Age about 3000 BC. Five hundred years later they and their neighbours in Redesdale and Coquetdale away to the north of us may well have embraced the old megalithic religion brought to them by missionaries from what's now southern Scotland. Later incursions by tribes from the wilderness in the north were less benign. We call them barbarians, but while the Votadini and Selgovae, the Novantae and northern Brigantes

caused their share of bother, I suspect we underestimate their Celtic talents for tribal organisation and diplomacy to the same degree that we've come to overstate the smartness of their Roman conquerors.

True, the Romans built a wall here grand enough to be a World Heritage Site. The sun reflects from the acres of visitors' cars at Housesteads Fort on the horizon to the north-west. But Hadrian's Wall perhaps isn't quite such an Imperial triumph as we were taught in the third form. There's as much justification for the view that it's a symbol of weakness and decline. The Roman Empire had overstretched itself by the time it arrived here. Hadrian's Wall was a line in the sands of time which said to the more expansionist generals – this far and no further. An eminent Romanist at one of the Northumbrian Universities once suggested to me that the Roman Empire was a bit like a Polo Mint. The sweet bits were all round the rim – places like this where economic growth was being generated by military activity.

Then of course came the Dark Ages. We know this because history books tell us so. After three hundred years or thereabouts of Roman Imperial adventure everything stopped. The Roman army turned on its jackbooted heel and marched out of Northumbria and back to Rome. Or rather it didn't. By that stage, certainly in the wall zone, you'd have been hard pressed to tell the difference between a Roman and a Northumbrian. The people living outside the forts were sisters or uncles of the soldiers inside. Some troops moved away to fight ever more preposterous continental campaigns but those left behind eventually tired of waiting for pay that never came, just went native, changed their line of business to protection racketeering and lived happily ever after. At least I hope they did. Without regular injections of Roman cash the population certainly declined and, in the Tyne Valley, didn't return to fifth-century levels until the Stephensons pushed the railway through Hexham fourteen hundred years later.

But far from the Roman twilight being the end of the glory days, Northumbria was about to experience its secular golden age as one of the most powerful of the Anglo Saxon kingdoms. Stretching from the Humber to the Clyde, it was actually two kingdoms united – Bernicia and Deira – and in its heyday in the sixth and seventh centuries Warden Hill was roughly at its centre.

Enter King Ida the Flamebearer, who in Anglo Saxon lore was but nine generations removed from the warrior god Woden. In AD 547 he built his royal capital on an abandoned Roman site on the Northumbrian coast, and founded a dynasty that made Bamburgh one of the great foundation stones of England. In myth Bamburgh was the Castle of the Joyous Gard given to Sir Galahad by King Arthur as a reward for defending Queen Guinevere's honour. The castle today is only slightly less fanciful than that – a confection; a recreation of history which soaked up a million pounds from the fortune of its restorer. He was Armstrong, the gunmaker who invented the best killing machine of Victorian times, the breech loading gun and who, it is tempting to imagine, must have had a touch of Woden in him too.

Northumbrians were and are by nature blunt, ambitious and individualistic. They've had another questionable advantage of possessing a territory rich in natural resources – coal, salt, navigable rivers, natural harbours and above all space. Invaders desired it and either sacked it or parcelled it up and gave it to their friends depending on whether they were Viking Danes or Norman French. The English and Scots institutionalised the belligerence, and modern Northumbria – essentially the counties of Northumberland and Durham with a bit of North Yorkshire tagged on – pushed as it was against a fiercely disputed national border, became a battleground.

The trenches of the Anglo-Scottish wars were at Berwick-upon-Tweed. It had been a Scottish borough but centuries of siege and attack shuttled it from kingdom to kingdom until in 1482 it became (at least at the time of writing) forever English. It was still in the front line during the time of Elizabeth I and the fortifications of Berwick – all £128,648.5s.9½d-worth of them – were the single costliest building project of her reign. The memory of Fortress Berwick's importance lingered on in Acts of Parliament until last century. When an Act specified where its rule would run, it would proclaim 'England, Scotland, Wales and Berwick-upon-Tweed'. And the town's Anglo-Scottish split personality continues in its football team. Berwick Rangers is the only English team to play in the Scottish League.

While armies of invasion or retribution were marching through the coastal flatlands of Northumbria, in the hills the broken men of the border Reiver riding surnames – Robsons (beware), Humes, Grays, Kerrs and Fosters – turned the protection racketeering of their Romano-British ancestors into a way of life. They were murderers and arsonists, kidnappers and cattle thieves. They left words such as bereaved and blackmail in the language. (At the time greenmail was a term for agricultural rent and blackmail was the money taken by night, in other words protection money.) The Elizabethan antiquarian Camden couldn't explore the central section of the Roman wall 'for the rank robbers thereabout'. Rankest of the lot were the Armstrongs camped out across the valley in the old Housesteads Fort. These borderlands between England and Scotland were the last part of mainland Britain to be pacified and the worst of the Reivers were transported to Northern Ireland (which perhaps explains a lot).

Here at another high viewpoint, the wind this time is whistling through the roofless Parthenon that's known as the Penshaw Monument. It was erected by public subscription in 1844 in memory of John George Lambton, first Earl of Durham. Known as 'Radical Jack' he was author of the first Reform Bill. His memorial on a hill between Chester-le-Street and Sunderland dominates a landscape that encapsulates Northumbria's past and future. The future, so the politicians and economists tell us, can be glimpsed in the sun reflecting from the windscreens in another car park. It's the back lot of the Nissan car works, one of the hi-tech, sunrise, inward investment industries on which these northern counties have pinned so much hope. There's an extraordinary coincidence in this image; a sense of history coming full circle. The man who has been credited more than any other with the industrialisation of Japan was Armstrong the gun-maker from Northumbria.

All around us are villages that once relied on coal for a living. The mines have gone. Not so long ago many of these communities were officially classified as Category D which, put more directly, meant that they would be allowed to die. To the east is the river Wear with its silent quaysides and the groans of an occasional rusting crane. The shipyards here, as on the Tyne and Tees, have gone. But though they've been replaced by business parks and marinas and supposedly desirable riverside housing developments, the soul of the place has been dislocated.

I'd gone to Penshaw with David Jenkins who was soon to retire as the barmy or visionary Bishop of Durham depending on which newspaper you read. My impression of him was of a gentle and erudite man whose cherubic smile disguised a streak of radicalism that made 'Radical Jack' seem like a dry-as-dust Tory. Ten years earlier, shortly after his appointment – an appointment that the Iron Lady would live to regret – he'd been brought to this place by his friend the Bishop of Jarrow so that, like Moses on Mount Pisgah, he could look out on his

Promised Land. What he saw terrified and invigorated him. There was much poverty and social turmoil. But on the far horizon was a symbol from which hope could spring.

For more than nine centuries Durham Cathedral has been Northumbria's inspiration. It's the greatest Romanesque church in all of Europe. It's an architectural triumph that springs from that conjunction of mathematics and mysticism that medieval builders knew as the Golden Cut. But more than all that, as the shrine of St Cuthbert it is a bridge to an age when Northumbria was the cultural capital of Europe. Here, for a time, was the fount of civilisation.

Christianity was spread throughout Northumbria by Aidan and a group of Irish monks in the early seventh century. They settled on the island of Lindisfarne – Holy Island – because it reminded them of their earlier home on Iona and also because it was close to the Christian King Oswald's royal residence at Bamburgh. Cuthbert was a shepherd from the Lammermuir hills who became prior and eventually Bishop of Lindisfarne. Much of his life was spent in self-imposed contemplative exile in his cell on the Farne Islands; he was bishop for just two years until his death on the 20 March 687, and yet his influence on the church and the people was immense. He helped to settle the long-running dispute between the Celtic and Roman rite in favour of Rome. And he was reputed to be a healer who drew pilgrims by the hundred during his lifetime and by the thousand after his death. It was the threat of Viking invasion that persuaded the monks of Lindisfarne that Cuthbert's body should be moved to a safer resting place. They travelled to Norham and Ripon and Chester-le-Street and eventually to Durham.

11

Cuthbert's reputation grew with the miles and the years. And the reputation of the Northumbrian kingdom similarly blossomed. Northumbria, the home of Caedmon, the herdsman who became the earliest English Christian poet; of Baeda – the Venerable Bede who in the monastery of Wearmouth and Jarrow wrote his *Historia Ecclesiastica* and by so doing became the Father of English History. It was monks from Northumbria who produced the finest illuminated manuscript of the age, the two hundred and fifty eight pages of vellum which are the Lindisfarne Gospels and it was a monk called Aldred from Chester-le-Street who translated their text from Latin into Northumbrian dialect thereby creating the earliest surviving English version of the Gospels. All this from a rough, remote, embattled kingdom in the north, somewhere up there behind the moors and mountains and hemmed in between the Pennines and the sea.

Northumbria still has its rough edges. Take a walk through Newcastle's Bigg Market on a Friday or Saturday night and allow yourself to be swept along on the tide of raucous, hedonistic, underdressed enjoyment and you'll see what I mean. Bits of it are still embattled, but the enemies now are poverty and social dysfunction. The only Viking invaders these days are the Scandinavian shoppers that come by the shipload to the port of Tyne Quay and after a raid on the Gateshead Metro Centre stagger back aboard with their cut price British plunder – everything from double beds to potato crisps.

Remoteness has become the mantra of the tourist brochures. But there are places where you can still experience a sense of the real isolation of Northumbria's past. Head for the hills beyond Kielder, where the biggest man-made lake in Europe laps the biggest man-made forest in Europe, and you're in a high, wild landscape that's much as it would have been in the days of Bede and Cuthbert. Go to Staithes on the coast between Redcar and Whitby and you'll find a village that not so long ago was still a closed community, accessible only from the sea unless you happened to know the smugglers' trails. More than half of the little houses piled precariously against the cliff were occupied by Verrills or Theeakers, accomplished fishermen who imbued the village's apprentice grocer James, later Captain Cook, with the ways of the sea.

Travel north to Chillingham near Wooler and you can find a link with the past that's as old as landscape itself. In a 350-acre walled park is a unique herd of wild white cattle, descendants of the beasts of pre-history that walked across the land bridge from Europe before Britain became an island. If you're prepared to accept myth and superstition as companions on your Northumbrian journey, Chillingham can supply those too in good measure. Chillingham Castle is reputed to be one of the most haunted places in Britain with visitations by ghosts as diverse as the radiant blue boy and the entire assembled court of King Henry VIII.

The spirit of Newcastle-upon-Tyne is rather more robust, its foundations rooted in the seam of coal that generated purpose and pride for seven centuries until it was decided that coal mining wasn't something that a proper, modern country should be doing any more. But the self-assurance and enterprise that were bred in the pits of the Northumberland coalfield find their most glorious expression in Newcastle. It can claim to be the only major city in England with a completely planned centre, the work, in the first half of the nineteenth century, of the architect John Dobson and the builder Richard Grainger. Against the odds, much of their work survives even though, in a fit of municipal madness, the architectural gem that was Eldon Square was pulled down to build a monstrous shopping mall.

I lived in Newcastle for almost ten years, working in a Dobson building – the old city lying-in hospital which had been taken over by the BBC and converted into Broadcasting House. When my BBC colleague Brian Redhead was writing about Northumbria some years ago he bemoaned the fact that one of his favourite buildings in Newcastle, the exquisite seventeenth-century Bessie Surtees house down by the river, had a shameful lack of public access because part of it was let off in flats. I have to confess that for a time I was one of the flat dwellers keeping the deprived public out. If Brian was still with us he'd no doubt be pleased to hear that the problem has been remedied, at least in part, because the house, in the shadow of the arching Tyne Bridge, is now the north-east headquarters of English Heritage and a bit of it is now open to the public.

Brian and I shared a fondness for another almost forgotten building in Newcastle. The city's Literary and Philosophical Society opened its doors in 1825 to satisfy the thirst for learning and self-improvement that was an obsession of the time. In a way it was a symbol of Northumbria's second age of enlightenment, a flowering of the arts and sciences that would leave its imprint

in many parts of the world. Here Sir Charles Parsons would explain the principles of his steam turbine, Sir Humphry Davy would talk about his revolutionary miners' safety lamp and Coleridge would come to hear him to 'increase his stock of metaphors'.

There's a meander through Northumbria that gives us a sense of the achievement and heady expectation of those times. Take the Alnmouth road, the old corn road that ran from Hexham the forty-odd miles to the port of Alnmouth and you'll find yourself rubbing shoulders with the thinkers, explorers and innovators of the age.

Cross the line of the Roman wall where in the mid nineteenth century the entrepreneurial town clerk of Newcastle, John Clayton, was spending his fortune on archaeological excavation. He bought all the forts between Chesters and Carvoran and gathered in the priceless collection of carved inscriptions and stone altars that would otherwise have been recycled as agricultural building materials and hard-core.

On to Wallington Hall where in the 1850s the Trevelyan family were playing host to a glittering array of painters and writers, among them Millais and Swinburne and Ruskin. They would take the air in the Wallington gardens which had been laid out by Capability Brown, the local lad from Kirkharle who went on to be gardener to King George III.

North to what's been described as Wagnerian Cragside where in the 1870s the by then Lord Armstrong spent another chunk of his armaments fortune turning 14,000 acres of Northumbrian hillside above the valley of the River Coquet into a pleasure ground and celebration of art and science and nature. He planted seven million trees. Cragside was the first house in the country to be completely powered by electricity. William Morris was employed to produce the stained glass for the library windows. Cragside encapsulates the achievements and contrasts of the Victorian age.

And so to Alnwick and the house of Percy. In the 1850s the fourth Duke of Northumberland, inheritor of the lands of Harry Hotspur, was in a building frenzy at Alnwick castle. The architect Anthony Salvin had been commissioned to turn the old place into an aristocratic vision of gothic chivalry with a dash of Italianate splendour. It was to cost the Duke a quarter of a million pounds. The old families certainly weren't going to allow themselves to be outdone by these coal and guns chappies. Wallington and Cragside are now in the care of the National Trust. The Dukes of Northumberland still hold sway in Alnwick castle.

For our final view of Northumbria let's imagine that it's a spectacularly bright day in the 1720s. We've climbed out 2676 feet to the summit of The Cheviot in the company of a rather strange fellow called Daniel Defoe who is collecting material for a volume that will certainly find its way into the grand libraries of Wallington and Cragside and Alnwick – *A Tour through the whole island of Great Britain.*

Following one of the many streams 'We mounted the hill as the besiegers approached a fortified town by trenches. The height began to look really frightful, for, I must own, I wished myself down again. The day happened to be very clear, and to our satisfaction very calm, otherwise the height we were upon would not be without its dangers.'

Steadying his nerve Defoe eventually dared to look out over what had once been the Kingdom of Northumbria. He claimed to be able to see the hills of Yorkshire and the eastern Lake District. There was the German Ocean twenty-two miles to the east; to the north Soutra near Edinburgh, and forty miles south the smoke from the salt pans of Shields at the mouth of the Tyne. He wasn't sure if he could see the Irish Sea or not but given that Port Patrick is 128 miles from The Cheviot it seems rather unlikely.

And then he was gone, anxious to get down to a safer altitude, which meant that I couldn't show him Windygyle where prehistoric chiefs are buried and the hanging stone and the hell hole where the fairies live and all the other secret corners of high, wild Northumbria.

ERIC ROBSON
February 1998

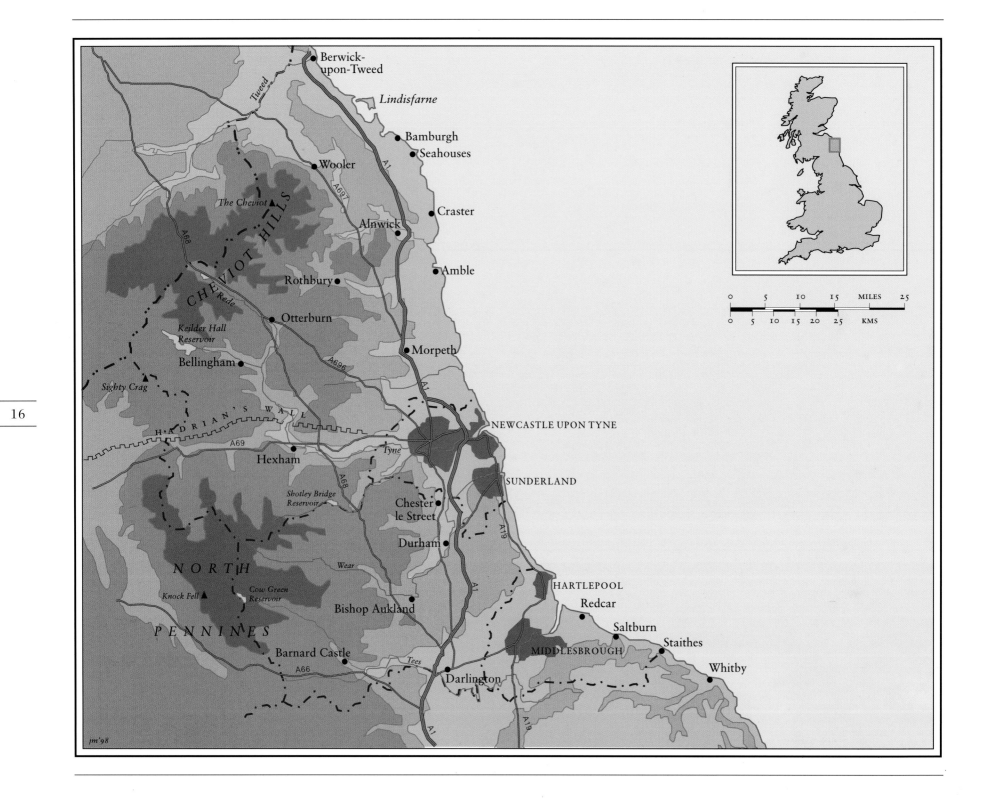

North Northumberland
and the Cheviots

Right: The fertile land of north Northumberland is ideal for agriculture, and from late spring onwards becomes a patchwork of lush green fields. This scene was captured near Chillingham where, on a clear day, you can see for miles in all directions and a wonderful sense of open space pervades.

Opposite page: The landscape of north Northumberland is dotted with small villages, among them Chillingham, Hepburn and Chatton. Chillingham is best known for its thirteenth-century castle which changed hands between the English and Scots through history and has now been fully restored to its former glory by Sir Humphrey Wakefield, a relative of the Grey family who originally built the castle. Chillingham is also home to a unique and rather fierce breed of wild cattle whose origins can be traced back beyond the twelfth century. This photograph shows Chatton with the Cheviots rising up on the horizon.

Right: With the Cheviot Hills on its doorstep, the old market town of Wooler in north Northumberland is a perfect base for walkers wishing to explore the nearby hills. Wooler can be seen on the far left of this photograph, which shows the town set in beautiful rolling countryside with the Cheviots in the background and the River Till in the foreground. Yeavering Bell, Northumbria's most impressive Iron Age hill fort, can be found a few miles to the west beyond Akeld.

Opposite page: Ford, north of Wooler, is one of Northumberland's prettiest villages. Noted for its picturesque cottages with their lovingly-tended gardens, Ford owes much of its beauty to Louisa, Countess of Waterford, who in the last century lived in nearby Ford Castle and spent a large part of her life turning it into a model village. A great artist, her biblical water-colours still line the walls of the school hall. Not far from Ford is Flodden Hill, site of a bloody battle in 1513 during which the Scots, under James IV, were defeated by the English. A memorial cross marks the battle site and is a poignant reminder of Northumberland's often bitter history.

Right: Not far from Wooler, Harthope valley cuts into the Cheviots. Formed by the Harthope Burn, which flows through a fault in the hills, visitors can explore the valley along a narrow road which travels through Earle as far as Langleeford. From there on it's walking country, with the summit of The Cheviot being the goal of most visitors.

Opposite page: Further south is the beautiful Breamish valley, where a river of the same name tumbles gently from the higher slopes. Set in the Northumberland National Park, the lower reach of the valley around Ingram provides a pleasant introduction to what's to come. Here the River Breamish, photographed at Bulby's Wood, can be seen on a perfect autumn day against the vibrant colours of the nearby hills.

22

Right: Access to visitors by car along the only road into the Breamish valley ends a couple of miles from Ingram at Hartside Farm. However, it's worth continuing on foot into the middle and higher reaches of the valley as the scenery just becomes more magnificent the further you go. This scene was photographed not far from Hartside Farm, looking towards the hamlet of Linhope.

Opposite page: Beyond Linhope the scenery quickly becomes much wilder and dedicated walkers can trek as far as the Scottish border. Along the higher reaches of the Breamish valley can be found the remains of Iron Age hill forts and medieval villages, signs that man has occupied this harsh landscape for thousands of years.

24

Right: The main attraction of the Breamish valley is Linhope Spout waterfall, which can be found three miles west of Ingram. However, the scenery encountered *en route* to the falls is even more breathtaking, especially in autumn, when the bracken-clad hills become a riot of rich, rustic colours. The narrow wooded gorge, above, is home to Linhope Spout.

Opposite page: Reaching the waterfall can be something of an anti-climax after walking so far. Said to be the most impressive in Northumberland (there are only two of note anyway, the other being Hareshaw Linn near Bellingham), it's not particularly big, or particularly impressive. Fortunately, the location is, and makes an ideal spot for a well-earned lunch break after the trek from Hartside Farm.

26

Right: The wildest and biggest of all the Cheviot valleys is that of the River Coquet, which flows from the upper reaches of the valley to the sea at Warkworth. The villages of Harbottle, close to where this stormy scene was captured, and Alwinton, provide ideal bases for exploring upper Coquetdale and the rugged Harbottle Hills.

Opposite page: As is common with the Cheviot valleys, only one road offering public access serves upper Coquetdale, and takes a meandering course along the riverside for twelve miles, deep into the hills. Not far from Alwinton is Uswayford Farm, shown here during a break in a dramatic autumnal storm. The handful of remote farms dotted through the valley are the only signs of human habitation in this uncompromising landscape.

To sample the best of upper Coquetdale it often becomes necessary to get away from the road into the hills themselves. Unfortunately, much of this area is used by the Ministry of Defence for artillery training, so access to the public is limited. Flags and signs posted through the valley show where and when access is permitted, though the sudden bursts of distant gunfire do nothing to instil confidence and most visitors never venture far from their cars. The scenes on the right and opposite were both photographed near Shillmoor.

Right: Not far from the site of the previous photograph are panoramic views across the bracken-clad hills into upper Coquetdale. Autumn is by far the best time of year in which to explore the valleys and hills of the Cheviots, as the wonderful colours in the landscape and the stormy, ever-changing light help to define the character of the region perfectly.

Opposite page: Leaving behind all signs of human habitation, the road through upper Coquetdale eventually begins a rapid climb until visitors are suddenly presented with a breathtaking vista back down through the valley and across the rolling Cheviots. This view, captured from the roadside beyond Shillmoor, must be one of the most memorable in the whole of Northumbria.

Right: At the far end of upper Coquetdale is Chew Green Roman Camp, where some of England's finest Roman earthworks can be found. To appreciate the scale of the camp you ideally need to trek up a nearby hill so it can be viewed from above, but the isolation of its location is ever-present, and it's hard to imagine legions of Roman soldiers living here so long ago. The road officially ends at Chew Green, though when the military ranges are clear, access to Rochester and Otterburn is possible.

Opposite page: Rothbury, the capital of Coquetdale and gateway to the Northumberland National Park, is a popular centre for walkers and holidaymakers. Set on the banks of the River Coquet, the town boasts a medieval bridge and an attractive main street of stone houses and shops. Nearby is Thrum Mill, where the Coquet is channelled through a narrow gorge.

Right: Just a mile or so east of Rothbury is Cragside, a magical Victorian estate now under the management of the National Trust. Built for the first Lord Armstrong, inventor of the Armstrong gun among other things, Cragside house is surrounded by 900 acres of parks and gardens with over 40 miles of scenic roads and paths. This combination of attractions makes it one of Northumberland's premier tourists sites – especially in early summer, when the gardens are ablaze with colour from the many thousands of rhododendron bushes.

Opposite page: Rothbury enjoys a remarkable setting, its houses creeping up the side of ancient sandstone terraces. Here the town can be seen from Lordenshaws, a windswept moor in the shadow of the imposing Simonside Hills on the edge of Harwood Forest. Formed by sand deposits over 300m deep, these hills are popular with walkers, and on clear days offer remarkable views across to the Cheviots.

Right: Lordenshaws was once home to an Iron Age hill fort. Thought to have been established around 350BC, remains of the round stone houses and facing stones at the eastern entrance are still clearly visible today, despite the ravages of time. The settlement's elevated position affords clear views of the surrounding countryside – this photograph was taken looking roughly due east from the eastern entrance.

Opposite page: The most remarkable relic to be found at Lordenshaws, just a short walk west of the Iron Age hill fort, is a huge horseshoe-shaped rock known locally as the 'cup and ring' stone. So-called because of the clear markings carved into its surface, archaeologists have yet to discover what the true meaning of the rocks and their markings are, though they are thought to date back at least 5000 years to the New Stone Age (Neolithic period). One theory is that the carvings are associated with trackways or viewpoints, and that they were intended to provide visitors in the area with messages. We may never know for sure, but standing at the rock, looking west to the Cheviots, it's a sobering thought to realise that man was doing the same thing in 3000BC and saw pretty much the same view as we do today.

During autumn, Coquetdale becomes an invigorating palette of rustic colours. Deciduous woodland stands shoulder to shoulder with coniferous plantations, creating a striking contrast between the lush greens and warm tones of the falling leaves, while banks of bracken glow like gold in the afternoon sunlight. These photographs on the right and opposite were both taken near the village of Hepple.

Right: Beyond Hepple the landscape begins to rise dramatically towards wild, windswept moorland, offering panoramic views back towards Coquetdale and across Harwood Forest before plunging down towards the village of Elsdon. This area is served by the B6341 road linking Rothbury with Otterburn, and is the perfect choice for a scenic drive.

Castles and Coast

England's most northerly town, Berwick-upon-Tweed has had a long and chequered history. Located on a peninsula between the sea and the River Tweed, it was officially in Scotland until 1174, and over the next three centuries changed hands a dozen times. Berwick today offers a lively mix of tradition and culture, as well as many historical reminders of its turbulent past including medieval ramparts and Britain's first military barracks, now a museum. The photograph on the right shows the view from the cobbled waterside walkway towards the seventeenth-century stone bridge which still carries traffic over the river into the town. The view on the opposite page of Berwick's waterfront bathed in golden evening sunlight was captured from the south side of the Tweed.

44

Situated off the coast of north Northumberland, and linked to the mainland by a tidal causeway, Lindisfarne, or Holy Island as it has been known since the eleventh century, was one of Europe's main centres of Celtic Christianity during the Dark Ages.

The first monastery was founded by an Irish monk, St Aidan, in the seventh century, after the convert King Oswald invited him to Northumbria to preach. More famous, however, was St Cuthbert, who was buried on Lindisfarne in 687. His remains now lie in Durham Cathedral after being removed from the island in 875 by monks fleeing a Danish invasion.

Perched atop a rocky crag known as Beblowe in the south of the island stands Lindisfarne Castle (English Heritage). Built in the 1540s, it was intended to protect the harbour from the threat of Scottish invasion, but never saw active service. After falling into a bad state of disrepair, it was eventually bought by Henry Hudson, founder of *Country Life* magazine, in 1902 and turned into a private home on his behalf by the architect Sir Edwin Lutyens. The castle's lofty position makes it clearly visible from all over the island. On the right is the view from the nearby pebble beach, and opposite the view from the harbour where lobster and crab fishermen still ply their trade.

Right: Lindisfarne Priory, (English Heritage) was built between 1083 and 1140 under the commission of the Bishop of Durham – the patterns etched into the columns are the same as those of Durham Cathedral. All that stands today are the remains of the gatehouse, the cloister and defensive walls. The gatehouse, built from red sandstone, is shown right, literally glowing in the last light of a summer's evening.

Opposite page: In clear weather, Lindisfarne Castle can be seen on the horizon from miles around. This view, taken at sunset, looks across Budle Bay near Bamburgh. A road known as the Wyndings leaves Bamburgh's main street and follows the coastline north for half a mile towards the golf course, where there are breathtaking views out to sea.

Right: The pretty coastal village of Bamburgh is dominated by its enormous castle, perhaps the most dramatic and perfect in Northumbria. The Great Whin Sill on which the castle stands has been used as a stronghold since the Iron Age, though the castle you see today, shown right, was begun by the Normans and added to over the following centuries. Lord Armstrong, who established the Cragside estate near Rothbury, purchased Bamburgh Castle in 1894 and carried out major restoration work.

Opposite page: The maze-like grassy sand dunes of Bamburgh provide welcome respite from the cold winds that often blow in from the North Sea, ripping across the extensive beach and pounding the village. Here the row of houses along the Wyndings, a narrow road skirting the beach, have an almost surreal appearance sandwiched between the dunes and sky.

50

Bamburgh Castle is at its most dramatic when viewed from the nearby beach which it overlooks. Low tide reveals a series of flat rocky shelves and leaves behind shallow pools that reflect the colours in the sky.

The photographs on the right and opposite were taken within minutes of each other on a stormy spring evening. The first shows a rainbow arching gracefully into the sky while the castle is illuminated by the last golden rays of light from the setting sun. Minutes later, with the sun sinking beneath the horizon, its light tinges storm clouds rolling in off the sea, as if they're about to engulf the castle and all that surrounds it. Northumberland has a quality of light all of its own: a constant joy and challenge to any photographer.

Right: The sweeping two-mile long sandy beach that curves around Beadnell Bay is the highlight of this quiet coastal town, and is a perfect place in which to get a feel for the wide open spaces and deserted beaches of the north Northumberland Heritage Coast – something you'd scarcely find anywhere else in England. Sand drifting against moored boats in the photograph on the right shows how the character of the coastline changes constantly with the wind. In the background is Beadnell's tiny harbour, the only one on the east coast which faces west, where you can usually find a boat or two sheltering behind the substantial walls.

Opposite page: Life buoys are a common feature along the Northumberland coast, and create eye-catching splashes of colour when juxtaposed against the blue sky. The one shown opposite was discovered while wandering along the beach at Beadnell Bay – where you can also catch glimpses of Dunstanburgh Castle thrown into sharp silhouette on the horizon.

Right: Seahouses is perhaps the only town along the north Northumberland coast where there are any real signs of tourism – and they are restricted to the odd amusement arcade or fish 'n' chip shop. Despite its popularity with tourists during the busy summer holiday season, however, it still manages to retain a relaxed air – and its character as a working fishing town complete with bustling harbour.

Opposite page: Covering an area of eleven acres, Dunstanburgh Castle (English Heritage) was once the biggest in Northumbria – and still is. Its isolated position is also the most impressive, conjuring up visions of knights in shining armour, damsels in distress and bloody battles.

Built in the early part of the fourteenth century by Thomas, Earl of Lancaster, it came under attack many times before falling into ruin in the sixteenth century. The best approach to the castle is along the coastal path from Craster, a mile or so to the south, from where the photograph opposite was taken. The beach at Embleton Bay to the north also gives superb views.

The tiny fishing village of Craster was once a busy port trading in whinstone, though today it is much quieter and famed mainly for its delicious kippers, which have been produced in the village for 150 years and are now exported all over the world. Craster's existing harbour, surrounded on three sides by pretty cottages, was built at the turn of the century by local landowners and is either bustling with local fishing boats – cobles – or empty because the men are out at sea. Another common sight for which Craster is renowned are the piles of colourful lobster pots stacked by the harbour stacked by the harbour.

Considered by many to have been the strongest fortress in England, Alnwick Castle has remained largely intact, despite the centuries of battles that ravaged many other Northumbrian castles and fortresses.

The seat of the Percy family since 1309, and home to the current Duke of Northumberland, Alnwick Castle is best appreciated from the banks of the River Aln close to the town centre, where the impressive walls and towers are often reflected beautifully in the calm waters of the river and visitors can enjoy peaceful strolls along the reed-clad banks. This location is reached over the imposing Lion Bridge, complete with its lead Percy Lion, which crosses the river below the town – see opposite page.

60

Right: The road from Alnwick to Rothbury passes through beautiful countryside where the Cheviot Hills are clearly visible in the distance and the landscape drops dramatically down Corby's Crags towards Holne Park and Thrunton Wood.

The photograph on the right shows an early morning view down the valley, while on the opposite page are the ruins of thirteenth-century Edlingham Castle. Situated near Edlingham Burn, all that remains of the castle today is a crumbling tower house and traces of a once grand fireplace.

From Alnwick, the meandering River Aln winds its way gracefully towards the sea at Alnmouth, sweeping *en route* past the village of Lesbury. The photographs on the right and opposite were both taken from a minor road linking Alnmouth with the tiny coastal village of Boulmer just a few miles away, and show the Aln in all its glory, cutting a swathe through the rolling landscape, right, and shimmering like a ribbon of gold at sunset, opposite page.

64

Perched by the banks of the Aln estuary yet only a stone's throw from a long, sandy beach, Alnmouth is an idyllic village where visitors come to enjoy the peace and quiet, or to practise their golf swing at the local club.

The photograph on the right shows Alnmouth's beautiful beach – virtually deserted at all times other than the peak of the summer holiday season – where uninterrupted sea views are on offer to visitors walking the sands. On the opposite page the Aln estuary at low tide is captured by the light of a summer sunset.

A storm in 1806 changed the course of the Aln and cut off the ruins of the nearby Norman church of St Waleric, set on a hill opposite the harbour. Fortunately, this area is still accessible by heading down a narrow, unsurfaced track off the coastal road towards Amble and walking along the dunes – see on the right. Do so and your effort will be justly rewarded with breathtaking views down the Aln estuary from Church Hill, as shown on the opposite page.

The village of Warkworth, built within a loop of the River Coquet, is dominated by Warkworth Castle which stands high above the river.

The earliest fortress on the site was of 'motte and bailey' construction and appeared around 1150, but by the late thirteenth century it had been replaced by a much grander building. In 1332 the Percys of Alnwick took over, the first Duke of Northumberland adding a three-storey keep in 1390 on the original motte, most of which can still be seen today – see photograph on the right.

In 1174 Warkworth was the site of a massacre: despite taking refuge in the castle, many of the village's inhabitants were murdered by the Scottish army. Thankfully, life in Warkworth is much quieter today, and there can be few scenes more memorable than the castle reflected in the calm waters of the Coquet – see opposite page.

Right: Just a mile or so south of Warkworth is the bustling fishing town of Amble, where the marina now mainly contains pleasure boats; but fishing trawlers still line the harbourside and nets are often laid out to dry in the sun as they have been for centuries. Amble is best enjoyed by following the Aln estuary from the harbour, along the marina and back towards Warkworth, where the castle can be clearly seen on the horizon.

72

THE TYNE TO THE TEES

Right and opposite: Newcastle-upon-Tyne, Northumbria's regional capital, is a vibrant, cosmopolitan city best known for its semi-circular bridge which arches across the Tyne. Once a Roman frontier town – Hadrian's Wall extended as far as the Tyne – Newcastle is home to many beautiful buildings, both old and new. The New Castle, originally built by William the Conqueror's illegitimate son, Robert Curthose, in 1080, offers excellent views of the city, but far more impressive is Grey Street, where a row of immaculate columned buildings descends towards the Tyne.

One of the best areas to visit is the Quayside, where you can take a relaxing stroll along the Tyne and admire the grandeur of its three bridges – sunset is an ideal time to do this. The Quayside also comes alive on a Sunday with its famous market.

74

Right: Smoking chimneys on the horizon can be seen for miles north and south of Teesmouth, and are a constant reminder of the industry that still goes on in the north east. Their appearance also seems rather at odds with the tranquillity of the Cleveland coastline – this picture was taken from the beach at Redcar, where the constant ebb and flow of the tide sculpts the flat sand into slender ripples.

Opposite: Set within an enormous loop of the River Wear, Durham is by far Northumbria's most spectacular city, and from any angle presents visitors with beautiful views. The old part of the city is best appreciated first by walking along the banks of the Wear between Framwelgate Bridge and Kingsgate Bridge, where the eleventh-century castle and cathedral can be seen towering above. Next, explore the narrow cobbled streets and square by crossing Kingsgate Bridge and walking up towards Palace Green. The remains of St Cuthbert of Lindisfarne found their final resting place in Durham in 995 after over a century of 'wandering' around Northumbria. The tomb of the Venerable Bede can also be found in the Cathedral's Galilee Chapel. This photograph, taken from the banks of the Wear near Prebends Bridge, shows the Cathedral with the old Fulling Mill, now a museum of archaeology, next to the weir.

Right and opposite: Saltburn-by-the-Sea on the Cleveland coast is an attractive seaside town with one of the few piers in the region cutting across a long sandy beach. Unlike the bigger resorts further along the coast in North Yorkshire, however, Saltburn shows few signs of the 'Kiss-me-quick' commercialism that has spoilt many beautiful towns, and retains a quiet, peaceful air – especially out of season, when the only people you are likely to see on the beach are locals walking their dogs.

These photographs show the view along the pebble beach towards the towering cliffs of Saltburn Scar, and the pier in golden early morning sunlight.

Right: The coastal scenery of Cleveland changes dramatically at Saltburn, where towering sea cliffs make an appearance and provide a welcome break from the relative flatness of the coast heading north towards Teesmouth. This photograph shows Saltburn Scar, which can be found at the eastern end of the town.

Opposite: A few miles south-east of Saltburn is the quiet coastal village of Skinningrove, where local fishermen moor their boats on the sand and pebble beach. This view, captured from the coastal path which forms part of the Cleveland Way, shows Cattersty Sands with Hunt Cliff in the background.

Right: The rocky pinnacle of Roseberry Topping (National Trust) is one of the most distinctive landmarks in Cleveland. Visible for miles around, it has played a significant role in the region's history. In the sixteenth century a beacon was positioned on the summit to warn of the approach of the Spanish Armada, and it later became the site of extensive quarrying and mining. A walk to the summit is recommended for wonderful views across the Cleveland Hills and Teesside.

Opposite: At 200m above sea level, Boulby Cliffs near Staithes are the highest in England and provide some of the most breathtaking views in the whole of Northumbria. The 108-mile Cleveland Way follows this area of coastline *en route* to Filey in North Yorkshire, and in places takes walkers to within metres of the cliff edge.

82

Right: A journey through Northumbria concludes, at least if country boundaries are to be observed, at the picturesque fishing village of Staithes. Although Staithes is situated in North Yorkshire, the beck flowing through the village to the sea – Roxby Beck – marks the border between Cleveland and North Yorkshire.

Staithes has served as a landing stage and fishing village for centuries, with local fishermen mooring their traditional craft – the flat-bottomed coble – along the beck. Captain James Cook served an apprenticeship in Staithes before finding fame by sailing his ship – *Discovery* – around the world.

THE NORTHERN PENNINES

Right: Set high above the River Tees to the west of Barnard Castle in County Durham stands Bernard's Castle. Parts of the original twelfth-century fortification are still visible, but most of the remains date from the fourteenth and fifteenth centuries. Barnard Castle itself is an attractive, bustling town, with wide streets and an eighteenth-century Market Cross of octagonal design. Bullet holes in the weather vane of the Market Cross are said to have been added during a shooting contest at the turn of the nineteenth century.

Opposite page: Barnard Castle's main attraction is the splendid Bowes Museum, which can be found on the approach into town from the south. Built in the latter part of last century to the design of a French chateau, it looks somehow out of place in the north of England, but is nevertheless an architectural masterpiece. A museum since it was opened in 1892 by John and Josephine Bowes, it contains one of Europe's finest private art collections.

Right: The lowlands of the Northern Pennines provide local farmers with large tracts of fertile land, and during the summer months fields of golden oilseed rape can often be seen shimmering in the sunlight. This photograph was taken near Greta Bridge, a few miles south-east of Barnard Castle.

Opposite page: Between Greta Bridge and Barnard Castle stand the romantic ruins of Egglestone Abbey. Founded by Premonstratensian Canons towards the end of the twelfth century, it was sold in 1548 and part of the cloisters were converted into an Elizabethan house. This too is now in ruins, but the view of the abbey, on a hill above the wooded banks of the Tees, is a memorable sight.

Right and opposite: Teesdale is at its most beautiful as you move north-west beyond Barnard Castle. The main road through this area, the B6277, follows the course of the river and rewards visitors with superb views down the Tees valley, where green fields touch the wooded banks of the river and villages climb up the distant slopes.

The countryside is still rather tame compared to what's just around the corner, and provides a gentle introduction to the beauty and grandeur of Upper Teesdale and the Northern Pennines.

90

Right and opposite: Beyond the old lead-mining town of Middleton-in-Teesdale the landscape becomes wilder and the river more dramatic. Over the Tees three miles north-west of the town is Wynch Bridge, Europe's first suspension bridge, and nearby a pretty series of shallow cascades known as Low Force. Far more impressive, however, is High Force which can be found 1½ miles further upstream. At this point the River Tees is squeezed through a gap in the Great Whin Sill, and drops more than twenty-one metres down a gully, creating the highest waterfall in England.

High Force is approached along a wooded path above the Tees and its roar can be heard long before you can see the falls. The photograph right was taken from above the falls, looking down the valley, while opposite you can see the Tees tumbling towards High Force from its higher reaches in the Pennines.

Right: Continuing onwards towards Forest-in-Teesdale the countryside takes on a more relaxed air, with pleasant views across Teesdale. This field of dandelions was photographed by the roadside near Forest-in-Teesdale. A little further on at Langdon Beck, a minor road heads south-west towards Cow Green Reservoir where visitors can walk to Cauldron Snout, England's longest cascade.

Opposite page: The grandeur of the Northern Pennines can be witnessed by leaving the main Teesdale road and heading up towards St John's Chapel over Harthope Moor. The road over this wilderness is the highest in England, and offers unmatched views across Weardale. This photograph was taken between Langdon Beck and St John's Chapel.

Right: Moving on north into the heart of windswept Weardale the landscape becomes ever wilder and it's impossible not to feel humbled by the vast, open landscape. The village of Rookhope makes an impressive sight, nestling between the lower slopes of the folding hills, while Stanhope Common and Middlehope Moor are dotted with lonely hill farms – like the one shown in this photograph, captured above Rookhope in the midst of a snowy January.

Opposite: The border between County Durham and Northumberland can be found high in the Northern Pennines near the village of Allenheads. The border is marked by a tall stone cairn high above panoramic views across the vast, empty landscape. This photograph was taken in freshly-fallen snow just metres from the border cairn.

96

Right: A mile or so over the Northumberland border is Allenheads, a tiny village set deep in a wooded valley. Allenheads was built primarily to house workers from the nearby East Allen mine and their families. Reminders of the lead mining industry, which eventually ground to a halt at the end of the last century, can be found at the Killhope Lead Mining Centre a couple of miles away, where a restored waterwheel over ten metres in diameter is the main attraction.

Opposite: Near Allenheads is Far Sipton Shield, where hill farms are scattered across the rolling countryside and it is so quiet that farmers can be heard from miles away as they call in their flocks from the hills. Life in the Northern Pennines is harsh; heavy snow can cut off whole villages for days on end and temperatures drop to well below freezing.

Right: Tucked away in a deep wooded valley, Blanchland is considered by many to be the most beautiful village in the county. Best-known for its picturesque stone cottages, many of which were built in the 1750s for the owner of the estate, Lord Crewe, Blanchland's origins go back much further. There's a fifteenth-century stone gatehouse in the village, while the abbey was founded in 1165 by Premonstratensian Canons. The best view of the village is from the bridge to the south – where this photograph was taken.

100

Hadrian's Wall Country

Right and opposite: Hadrian's Wall, originally running seventy-three miles (eighty Roman miles) from the Solway Firth in the west to Newcastle and the Tyne in the east, is the most significant reminder of Roman occupation left in England today. Built between 122 and 130 under the command of Emperor Hadrian, its aim was to create a fortified barrier with which the Romans could prevent invasion from Scottish tribes, and control the movements of the so-called barbarians who came into the area to trade.

In the photograph on the right, a straight section of the wall can be seen heading off towards Walltown in the west of Northumberland. On the opposite page is part of the Great Whin Sill at Cawfields (National Trust) on which the most impressive sections of Hadrian's Wall were built. This striking geological feature was formed almost 300 million years ago when molten rock was pushed up through the earth's crust.

Right: The best preserved and most dramatic sections of Hadrian's Wall are to be found between Cawfields and Housesteads, where the wall follows the Great Whin Sill and hugs the graceful contours of the landscape. This photograph was taken from Steel Rigg (National Trust), looking east at sunrise towards Crag Lough and Hotbank Crags, with the whin sill clearly visible.

Opposite page: Sunrise and sunset are undoubtedly the best times to experience the drama and beauty of Hadrian's Wall. This section was photographed just west of Steel Rigg, close to Milecastle 40. In its heyday, Milecastles were positioned every Roman mile along the wall and as well as providing lookouts, they also allowed the Romans to extract a toll from anyone wishing to pass through. Between eight and thirty-two men were stationed in each Milecastle.

104

Right: Between Steel Rigg and Housesteads the wall passes over relatively high terrain, giving wonderful views across surrounding countryside. This photograph is looking south from the wall above Sycamore Gap (National Trust).

Opposite page: Once up to three metres thick and over six metres high, Hadrian's Wall quickly fell into disrepair after Emperor Hadrian's death in 138. His successor abandoned the wall in favour of pushing north into Scotland, and although the Romans eventually returned in 160, over the next two centuries the wall was overrun on several occasions, mainly by the Picts. Finally, in 383 the Romans withdrew from Britain for good, leaving the wall to the mercy of man and the elements. This photograph shows the wall following the contours of the rolling landscape near Hotbank Crags (National Trust).

106

Right: The landscape around Housesteads and Twice Brewed is boggy and windswept, with crumbling barns and dark pools thrown in for good measure. This scenery is best viewed towards the end of the day, when golden sunlight rakes across the countryside, casting long shadows.

Opposite page: A walk along Hadrian's Wall from Steel Rigg towards Sycamore Gap and Crag Lough will be rewarded with incredible views east and west. Sycamore Gap, seen in the left of this photograph, gets its name from the fact that a single sycamore tree grows in a dip by the wall.

Right: One of the most popular places along Hadrian's Wall is Cuddy Crag, less than a mile west of Housesteads, where the wall can be seen for miles snaking along the top of the Great Whin Sill. This photograph was taken from Cuddy Crag as the light was fading at the end of a freezing winter's day.

Opposite page: Known to the Romans as Vircovicium, Housesteads Fort (English Heritage) is the best-preserved site on Hadrian's Wall, not only for the extensive remains that visitors can explore, but also for the breathtaking views its lofty position commands – Vircovicium means 'hilly place'.

Originally built in the second century AD to defend Knag Burn, though most of the existing remains are from the third and fourth centuries, Housesteads was once home to some 1000 soldiers.

110

Right: The small village of Wall, so-named because of its proximity to Hadrian's Wall – Chesters Roman Fort is only a mile or so away – has a pretty green surrounded by cottages of mellow stone. Like many of the villages in Northumberland, it remains relatively untouched by the advance of time.

Opposite page: It only takes one cold, clear night to transform the landscape of Northumberland into a winter wonderland, though the weather isn't as extreme as some may expect given the county's northerly position. This scene was photographed above Chesters Roman Camp from the hamlet of Walwick.

Right: One of the great joys of Northumberland is that the scenery never disappoints. Even wrong turns down unmarked lanes are usually rewarded before long with views across wild, open countryside – like this one, on Melkridge Common, just north of Hadrian's Wall between Cawfields and Twice Brewed.

Opposite page: The countryside immediately south of Hadrian's Wall around Housesteads and Steel Rigg is relatively flat, which means the sun continues to shine almost until the moment it sets, adding an incomparable golden glow to the landscape. For landscape photographers, the last hour of daylight is usually the best and a battle against the clock always ensues in order to make the most of it.

114

Right and opposite: Set in the heart of Tynedale, Hexham is an attractive town with a long and fascinating history. The town's first priory was built around 650 and parts of it, such as Wilfrid's Crypt, still exist in the twelfth-century abbey that dominates the skyline today.

There are many more reminders of the past too, such as the fourteenth-century Moot Hall, the Archbishop's Gaol and the narrow cobbled streets. Many of Hexham's older buildings were constructed using stone from nearby Roman ruins – a practice that became common once the Romans left Britain towards the end of the fourth century AD.

Right: The town park in Hexham, opposite the Abbey, comes to life in autumn when leaves on the towering deciduous trees turn from lush green to vibrant yellows, oranges, reds and every shade in between. The nearby riverside country park of Tyne Green is also well worth a visit at this time of year for the amazing show of colour along the banks of the River Tyne.

KIELDER AND THE NORTH TYNE

Right: The impressive stone bridge over the River North Tyne at Chollerford, four miles north of Hexham, stands not far from the site of Chesters Roman Camp (Cilurnum). Chesters was built to protect Hadrian's Wall at the point where it crossed the North Tyne. Remains of the original Roman bridge over the river, and its successor, which was built around the turn of the third century AD, can still be seen today.

Opposite page: The River Tyne is made up of two main arteries – the South Tyne, which flows south of Hadrian's Wall, and the North Tyne, which heads down from Kielder Water. The two converge a few miles north of Hexham before flowing west towards Newcastle and Tynemouth. This photograph, taken from Chesters Bridge, shows the gentle North Tyne flowing between tree-lined banks at Chollerford; an idyllic scene on an idyllic day.

Right: Perched above the east bank of the River North Tyne near Wark, Chipchase Castle enjoys a magnificent position with views across surrounding countryside. Its origins go back to the fourteenth century, from which date a tower with corner turrets still remains. The castellated Jacobean mansion was added in the 1620s and is one of the finest examples of architecture from that period in Northumberland.

Opposite page: The rolling countryside around the North Tyne between Wark and Kielder, like most of Northumberland, comes to life during autumn when the acres of deciduous woodland and banks of bracken tinge the landscape with reds and golds. This scene was photographed near Redesmouth on a typically calm, clear autumnal day.

Right: The River North Tyne is hidden from view for much of its passage towards the Tyne by dense banks of trees, with occasional glimpses appearing through breaks in the woodland. This picture was taken near Wark, where the road north to Bellingham and beyond follows the course of the river and footpaths allow visitors to get much closer to the water's edge.

Opposite page: Bellingham, just visible in the distance in this photograph beneath a blanket of light mist, is the gateway to Kielder and the Border Forest Park.

The capital of North Tyne, Bellingham boasts a fascinating history. The remains of St Cuthbert, removed from Lindisfarne by retreating monks in the ninth century, spent time here *en route* to their eventual resting place in Durham, and through the sixteenth and seventeenth centuries the small town often found itself at the hands of bands of robbers, known as Reivers.

Right and opposite: The main attraction in Bellingham is Hareshaw Burn, a gently flowing stream which tumbles over rocks and ledges in a densely wooded valley on the edge of the town. A footpath follows the course of the burn for a mile or so upstream to Hareshaw Linn, an attractive waterfall set in a rock amphitheatre. The walk is actually more satisfying than the falls: on a quiet morning the only sounds you're likely to hear are those of the burn itself and the wide variety of birds that inhabit the woodland.

Right: Towards Kielder Water the valley of the North Tyne becomes much wider and flatter, and offers clear views over to farmhouses dotting the surrounding hills. This area is on the edge of the Border Forest Park, which covers more than 200 square miles and is an important habitat for wildlife – as well as being a popular place for leisure activities such as walking and cycling along the miles of wooded paths.

Opposite page: Kielder Water, Europe's largest man-made lake, is set in the heart of the Kielder Forest with coniferous plantations reaching down to its shores. The scale of the lake has to be seen to be appreciated. Nine miles long, and with almost thirty miles of shoreline, it holds 40 million gallons of water and has a surface area of over 2,500 acres. This photograph was taken from Elf Kirk, on the south side of Kielder – the tiny yachts in the distance offer a clue to just how big the area is.

Right: North of Bellingham the rolling countryside quickly becomes windswept moor and heathland, home to sheep and a scattering of hill farms. On clear days you can see for miles towards north Northumberland as the road climbs high before dropping down towards Otterburn.

Opposite page: Otterburn is a quiet place set on the banks of the River Rede – shown in this photograph near the outskirts of the town. Its main claim to fame is far less romantic than the gentle waters of the Rede, however, for it was the site of one of Northumberland's bloodiest battles – the Battle of Otterburn. In 1388 the English, under the command of Harry Hotspur, clashed with Scottish soldiers led by Earl Douglas. In the moonlight battle that ensued Douglas was killed and Hotspur himself was taken hostage by the conquering Scots.

The skulls and bones of over 1000 men, discovered in nearby Elsdon churchyard last century, are said to be the remains of dead soldiers carried there after the battle.

Right: Beyond Otterburn the landscape rises into open moorland where dry stone walls stretch unbroken for miles. Access into this area is unfortunately restricted as it's used for live firing practice by the Ministry of Defence. North-west of Otterburn the activity is particularly intense, and it is common to see the red warning flags fluttering in the wind.

When the flags are down, access is permitted, and you can follow moorland roads and paths across country to the Coquet valley in the Cheviot Hills. The route to Chew Green Roman Camp near the Scottish border is particularly memorable. It can be reached by turning off the A68 north-west of Rochester. From Chew Green the narrow road then travels for twelve miles through breathtaking upper Coquetdale to Alwinton.

132

Until I was approached to take the photographs for this book, my only experience of Northumbria, like that of most people, had been fleeting glimpses from a speeding car on the A1, *en route* to Scotland. Now, having spent the best part of a year exploring the region, in all seasons and all types of weather, I have to say it ranks as my favourite place for landscape photography. Nowhere else in England will you find such scenic diversity. From the rolling hills of the Cheviots and the amazing spectacle of Hadrian's Wall, to the beautiful, unspoilt coastline of North Northumberland and the wild openness of the Northern Pennines, Northumbria has something for everyone, and I feel confident in saying that, like me, once you have set foot over the border you will yearn to return again and again.

Photographing Northumbria required careful planning to ensure that all corners could be explored and that I didn't miss any important locations. That said, being such a vast area – the region takes in the counties of Northumberland, Tyne & Wear, Cleveland and County Durham – it was always going to be impossible to cover everything in one book, and I apologise for any omissions which you feel perhaps deserved inclusion.

The most important aspect of landscape photography for me is light. Without good light, it becomes impossible to capture the true beauty and character of a scene on film. Consequently, much of my time in Northumbria was spent watching the weather and waiting. It takes a mere fraction of a second to record a photograph, but hours, even days of waiting often precede that moment.

The vast majority of photographs in this book were taken with a Pentax 67 medium-format camera and 55mm, 105mm, 135mm, 165mm and 300mm lenses, particularly the 55mm wide-angle as its field-of-view and perspective match my own way of 'seeing'. I favour the 6x7cm format both for its superb image quality, and also because I prefer composing landscape pictures in a rectangular format. The Pentax 67 was chosen because it's a robust, manual camera that can withstand the rigours of daily use, often in harsh weather conditions.

The panoramic images were taken with a Fuji G617 panoramic camera and fixed 105mm lens. This elongated format doesn't suit all types of landscape scene, but my initial experiments with it are promising, and I hope to make better use of it in the future. As neither camera has integral metering, I carry two handheld meters – a Minolta Autometer IVF which allows me to measure the incident light falling on a scene, plus a Pentax handheld digital spotmeter which I use to take meter readings from a tiny part of the scene – usually a mid-tone such as green grass or foliage. My choice of film was Fujichrome Velvia which, at ISO50, is relatively slow. However, no other film offers the same combination of sharpness, clarity, near-invisible grain and such vibrant colours.

Like most photographers, I use filters in my work, though only to enhance what Mother Nature has already given me and never to try and make a 'silk purse from a sow's ear'! A polarising filter is often chosen in sunny weather conditions, to deepen blue sky, remove glare from foliage and eliminate reflections in water. The overall effect is that colour saturation is increased and clarity improved immensely. I also use a polariser for woodland scenes, even in dull weather, as it helps to intensify the colours in the foliage.

I also use a variety of neutral density (grey) graduated filters, to bring the brightness of the sky in line with that of the landscape so both are correctly exposed. Without a grad filter, the sky tends to 'burn out'. Finally, I often reach for a warm-up filter, not only to enhance the warmth of natural daylight, but also to balance the slight coolness that polarising filters tend to introduce. An 81B or 81C filter will usually combat that to give natural colour rendition.

A consequence of using slow-speed and light-sapping filters such as polarisers is that exposure times are almost always long. Even in bright sunlight I often find myself working at ½ second or more, especially with my lens stopped down to f/16 or f/22 to give increased depth-of-field. At dawn and dusk – my favoured times of day – exposures may run into many seconds. A tripod is therefore essential to prevent camera shake, though I also use one – a battered but sturdy Gitzo model – to aid composition. Handholding the camera tends to instil a quick-fire approach to photography, but by introducing a tripod into the equation the picture-taking process is slowed down and you tend to spend more time thinking about each picture.

The only item remaining is my trusty backpack in which all this equipment is carried. I use a LowePro Photo Trekker backpack. Despite being much slower to access than a conventional 'gadget' bag, it makes carrying heavy equipment for long periods much easier and infinitely more comfortable by distributing the weight of the outfit evenly across both shoulders.

Ultimately, of course, the equipment you choose for landscape photography is secondary. Of far more importance is your willingness to get out there and explore your surroundings, no matter how bad the weather is or how uninspired you feel. There's an old saying among landscape photographers that the harder you work, the luckier you get. I couldn't agree more.

LEE FROST

January 1998